I0036928

Investing

Investing In The Stock Market, Foreign Exchange, Day
Trading, And Options How To Build A Life Off Of Trading
And Make Money Online With Moneymaking Tactics That
Will Set You Free Financially

*(The Application Of Technical Analysis To The Financial
Markets)*

Aneas Zotter

TABLE OF CONTENT

Creating A Portfolio Consisting On Dividend Stocks

If you are just starting off, you might be wondering how you can initiate and expand your dividend portfolio in order to ensure that you get the most out of your passive income. In the same way that you would start with tiny positions when trading stocks, you will need to gradually expand over these as time goes on.

The primary objective of a portfolio focused on dividends is to maximize the growth of one's dividend income in proportion to the portfolio's total stock market value. Reinvesting your profits in the company through a strategy known as DRIP is one approach to accomplish this goal. The abbreviation "DRIP" refers to the Dividend Reinvestment Plan. It is a term that denotes a collection of directives and protocols that make it possible for you to reinvest in your stock firm by purchasing additional shares. This approach operates in never-ending loops that make it possible for your investment to increase in value. The more money you put back into your business, the faster your dividends will grow.

Selecting a broker that charges cheap trading fees and commissions is something else that you need to do if you want to increase the size of your portfolio. There are a few brokerage accounts that do not charge any commission fees, so you will be able to make trades with those. Making sure that the commissions are as low as they can be will go a long way toward ensuring that you do not spend all of the earnings from your investments on payments that are not essential. It is in your best interest to get the most potential profit out of each and every dollar that you put into dividend stocks.

When it comes to dividend allocation, you absolutely need to have a strategy that may give you a competitive advantage across the board with regard to dividend stocks. Here is an illustration of a dividend distribution strategy that has been successful for the vast majority of investors.

Dividend kings should make up 20% of the portfolio's total value. These are businesses that have maintained a pattern of annual dividend growth throughout the course of the past half century. This category contains a very limited number of businesses everywhere in the world.

Invest 35% of your money in dividend-paying stocks to build up your portfolio. Companies considered to be aristocrats are those that have maintained a consistent dividend growth rate for at least 25 years. This is due to the fact that the performance of such companies on the stock market is almost usually fairly consistent.

Invest 30% of your capital in stocks that will soon be paying dividends. These are stocks that have a proven track record of not just paying their shareholders but also consistently growing the dividends they pay out. Although these stocks are not as steady as dividend aristocrats and dividend kings, they are still very attractive investments.

The remaining 15% of the portfolio can be invested in overseas growth stocks. You can typically find these in global dividend growth funds or stocks made available by blue-chip international firms.

A major portion of your dividend portfolio should be allocated to aristocrats for the simple reason that these stocks have an outstanding history of both performance and success. Even though the returns from these stocks develop at a somewhat sluggish pace, Dividend Kings is another excellent choice.

When you are putting together a portfolio of dividend stocks, you should aim to have between 25 and 30 distinct stock types represented. You may start off with a relatively modest investment and gradually build up your holdings as you get experience with the process of trading such equities. Once you have a well-defined portfolio, you will be able to continually reinvest any returns you receive until you reach your objective. This method of reinvestment functions in a manner that is analogous to that of interest that is compounded over time.

This is due to the fact that, if you continue to reinvest your earnings, your potential income will increase at an exponential rate.

When carrying out this strategy, you should steer clear of placing all of your investment cash in a single sort of dividend stock. Be sure to spread your investments out over a variety of firms, industries, and market segments. If you do this, you will greatly reduce the risks associated with your investments, while simultaneously increasing the potential for you to amass riches.

The process of rebalancing

You are likely to discover, as time passes, that certain components of your investment portfolio increase at a faster rate than others. As a consequence of this, you can discover that your investment portfolio is not moving you closer to your objectives over the course of time. It's possible that you'll need to rebalance your portfolio in order to get it into the shape that you need it to be in so that you can use it effectively. This may require the sale of some investments, followed by the reinvestment of the proceeds in other types of investments.

People that utilize rebalancing are, for the most part, individuals who are employing an investment portfolio that consists of general classes of investments. Let's say, for the sake of argument, that you have a quarter of your entire investing capital in the form of cash and bonds. The remaining 50% of your portfolio may be invested in riskier, higher-growth companies, while the remaining 25% would be secure dividend equities. You might discover, at the end of the next year, that the piece of your portfolio that was invested in aggressive growth stocks expanded a great deal more quickly than the other sections of your portfolio. You should consider rebalancing the portfolio if the initial distribution was suitable for your investment objectives in general and you do not wish to increase the amount of risk you are taking by investing more of your money in stocks with aggressive growth potential.

Let's imagine that after a year, now 60% of your portfolio is invested in stocks with fast growth, 20% is invested in stocks that pay dividends, and 20% is invested in cash and bonds. You would need to sell off some of the aggressive growth stocks in order to keep the same balance in your portfolio. After that, you would put the earnings back into cash, bonds, and dividend stocks so that it would be back in its original proportions of 50-25-25.

"Portfolio drift" is the term used to describe the tendency of a portfolio to have more of its weight go into one asset class as opposed to another. Rebalancing is done with the intention of reducing overall portfolio risk rather than maximizing return on investment. When you initially design the asset allocation that will be employed in your portfolio, you should have done so with your goals and your level of tolerance for risk in mind. A more conservative asset allocation may be appropriate for some persons given their personal circumstances. The consensus among *financial counselors is that as people get older, they should adopt a more cautious approach to their finances. Naturally, the answer to this question is going to change depending on the circumstances. The hypothetical situation that the financial experts are considering is one in which a person completes their education at the age of 23 and immediately begins a foolproof investment strategy that will endure for at least three decades. We have explored the issue of older investors who need to play catch up because, unfortunately, not many people these days fit that criteria. As a result, the topic of older investors who need to play catch up was brought up in our conversation. If you find yourself in such a predicament, switching to a more conservative investing strategy is not the most effective way to handle the situation at hand.*

When you have your sights set on new financial horizons, naturally, your goals will shift, and you may discover that the new arrangement serves you better. This is a perfectly natural occurrence. Some investors may come to the conclusion that they require a more aggressive asset allocation than they originally anticipated, and as a result, they may choose to alter their course of action.

You should feel as like you are being held captive by your previous asset allocation as time passes and as your ambitions shift. You should make it a habit to check in on the relationship that exists between the risks you take and the potential rewards you reap on a regular basis, and consider how these factors interact with the dynamic aspects of your life.

The frequency with which you should rebalance your portfolio is a topic that frequently comes up in conversation. When it comes to rebalancing your investment portfolio, some financial consultants recommend doing so on a monthly basis, while others recommend doing so on a semi-annual or even annual basis. Although this is a matter of personal opinion, it is safe to say that the majority of people will benefit most from rebalancing their portfolio either annually or once per year. Although it is possible, it is quite improbable that a stock will surge by such a significant amount over the course of one month. However, it is not impossible. There is also the possibility of tax complications arising; however, if you rebalance your portfolio once a year, you can lessen the impact that this has.

If you are just starting out in the world of investing, there are a few often asked questions to which you might still require answers. The ten most frequently asked questions and our responses to them are listed below.

Do you need a large initial investment to get started with investing?

You do not, in fact. It is essential that you invest money that you are ready to bear the loss of in the event that something goes wrong. On the other hand, you should have no trouble finding a broker who would work with you to establish a little investment.

Do you think it would be beneficial to work with a financial advisor?

You absolutely should. Will you continue to rely on this financial advisor in the future? No. However, you should discuss the topic of diversification, the age at which you can retire, and your existing income with a financial counselor. Your financial advisor may be able to provide you with recommendations that you have not yet considered. If you have someone presenting advise to you, that does not imply that you have to take all of the advice that is given to you.

Where can you find the most reliable places to put your money?

Mutual funds are the most secure type of investment due to the fact that they are always being monitored and represent a variety of business sectors. You can also make investments in real estate, Roth IRAs, and 401Ks. These kinds of investments can be safer than trying to day trade or figure out which stocks are the greatest for long-term investing.

Is there any kind of assurance that your investment will result in a profit?

No, not even Warren Buffet can promise he would always make a profit from his investments. On the other hand, if you carefully study and research stocks, you will have a greater chance of making a profit than of suffering a loss.

What are some key indicators that help to determine the overall health of a stock?

Indicators of a stock's overall health include its earnings per share, price earnings ratio, and price to book ratio, among other metrics. These are the three ideas that financial experts consider when determining whether or not a stock is undervalued or overvalued.

Where can you look for research on different stocks?

The most effective solution is to invest money in a program or work with a broker to acquire access. The majority of brokers offer stock research, which typically includes RSS feeds for keeping up with company news as well as world news. You may determine facts about the worldwide sector, the industry a firm is a part of, as well as the specific company by using this research.

Should you subscribe to the local newspaper?

There were once a number of newspapers that were particularly useful for stock market investing. At this time, a significant portion of the information can only be obtained through your broker. Investors of a certain age feel that there is always something interesting to read in the Wall Street Journal. You might also be interested in the daily online edition of IBD, which is known as Investors Business Daily. Their daily newspaper has been reduced to a weekly edition that contains just old news.

What kind of a return can you anticipate from your investments?

The profit-to-loss ratio is not the same thing as the return on investment. The proportion of successful traders to unsuccessful ones is referred to as the profit-to-loss ratio. Returns on investments normally range between 7 and 8 percent for investors who are just starting out. This indicates that you should be able to make a profit of 7 to 8 percent for the entire year. Some people are fortunate enough to get a return on investment of 10 percent.

Should you invest even if you are experiencing fear?

You need to evaluate whether or not your anxiety will impact how you sleep, what you eat, and the amount of time you spend worrying about your investment. Fear is an emotion, and you need to remain logical and level-headed in this situation. However, you have the ability to choose investing opportunities that correspond to your level of comfort with risk. There are equities with low risk that have the potential to generate modest returns.

What are the reasons behind your lack of success in the stock market?

This is a question that is asked by everyone, and there are a lot of different explanations for why someone might be having difficulties. It's possible that their entry/exit strategy was formulated wrongly. They could also be attempting to adjust their stop orders in the hopes of improving their earnings, even while they are losing money. It is time for you to read this book again, learn advanced investing tactics, and avoid making the mistakes that are the most prevalent among individuals. If you are losing money or not making money, it is time for you to read this book again.

The Mercantile Kit As It Were

Every person should have a collection of tools for their work. There is no exception to this rule when it comes to being a trader. In order to become an investor in penny stocks, you will require a tool kit that will allow you to hone your skills and trade tiny stocks profitably. In a nutshell, it increases the likelihood of your accomplishments being successful.

Websites like are some of the most user-friendly solutions available. Checking the percentage of people that gained weight with this tool is quite easy, and it is completely free. However, due to the fact that this is a free tool, there is a possibility that the results may not be as precise as desired. This is because less time and effort is spent ensuring that the results are correct.

You are welcome to make advantage of this additional fantastic free tool. As a trader, you can make advantage of the simplified charts and other forms of information that are provided by this resource. There is also a paid edition accessible, so if you enjoy the free version sufficiently, you might want to think about upgrading to the paid one. This is especially the case if you are interested in learning about all of the financial qualifications associated with a particular quantity of stock.

This is a platform that is managed by the Worden brothers and is recognized as the primary support system for the TC-200 200 software. It is really helpful for performing technical analysis, and if you upgrade to the premium edition, you can even obtain access to more detailed information. Again, this entirely depends on the size of your financial investment, but it is a good idea to think about investing in tools that will make your life simpler when it comes to conducting research and analysis of a certain stock. Because of this, you will be able to recognize more chances and threats along the way, which will make your journey more successful.

It is a terrific charting tool, and once again, the premium edition offers deeper details than the free version does. This is to be expected, as the makers would like to earn some money from the equipment theory they are producing.

This is an excellent site that allows you to search for and keep an eye out for specific SEC filings that you are aware of looking for. In addition, this is a trustworthy website, which means that you will most likely discover what you are looking for here. There is nothing that can be more detrimental to a person's success than relying on information that is not reliable, which is why it is best practice to always verify the accuracy of the trading tools and sources that you use.

This is a website where one can acquire suggestions for trading various kinds of equities.But you should be careful about who you put your faith in when utilizing this site, and you should never trade on the trading idea of another person unless you completely grasp their technique and come to the same conclusion on your own. It is beneficial to glean ideas from individuals who have been involved in the industry for a longer period of time, but in the end, it is your own money that is at stake. As a result, it is strongly recommended that you continue to maintain responsibility for any plans that you carry out.

If you want rapid access to other websites that provide information on stock and essential data, this is a fantastic tool that you can use. It is handy if you want to utilize it. In a nutshell, it is an excellent research instrument that may assist in providing you with the information that you require.

You can use this fantastic and totally free piece of software to figure out the candlestick patterns that you have learnt in the s that came before this one. It should come as no surprise that this is a valuable resource for doing an analysis of the opening and closing stock prices of a specific firm.

The following is a list of some of the most common tools that are required for investing in penny stocks and that you should most definitely consider adding to your toolkit:

Screeners for stocks. These have the ability to analyze the entirety of the market and provide data such as the typical trade volume, chart patterns, and other relevant information.

Software for creating charts. This demonstrates how a stock, fund, or index has performed over a given period of time.

Simulations of stock markets. This is a platform that allows you to practice fundamental analysis or even test out trading techniques without having to necessarily spend the money. It is ideal for novices, especially, because it does not require you to spend money. You can also work on the simulations while you are actually trading, particularly for the purpose of testing out new methods that you may have invented or the ideas of others, to see how well they work out. Keep in mind that the simulation does not take all of the costs into account and that it does not account for the emotional component.

The exchange of newsletters. Traders receive these alerts, typically in the form of emails or printed bulletins, to inform them of odd market moves, new developments, and innovations. In the world of investments, being current is really important, particularly when attempting to forecast the overall success that may be achieved. In addition to this, it offers the thoughts of industry professionals regarding the movements that stocks ideally will make in the future as well as which stocks have the most potential. Now, further study may need to be acquired in order to discover the opinions of the industry professionals on penny stocks.

The Workings Behind Bitcoin

The objective of the libertarians who were a part of the cypherpunk movement was to create a kind of digital currency that could be used in the electronic digital age but still maintained the same degree of anonymity as paper currency, which was something that they valued. This was made very evident in the "manifesto" that they published:

"There is no need to know who I am when I make a transaction at a store, such as when I buy a magazine and hand the cash to the clerk. My electronic mail provider does not need to know to whom I am speaking, what I am saying, or what others are saying to me in order to send and receive messages for me; my provider only needs to know how to get the message there and how much I owe them in fees........ Therefore, the use of anonymous transaction systems is necessary for protecting privacy in open societies. Cash has been the predominate form of this system up until this point. A transaction system that is anonymous is not the same as a transaction system that is secret. Individuals have the ability, inside an anonymous system, to expose their identify when they want to and only when they want to; this is the core of privacy.

2. Financial Stability

To summarize, the "Sound Money" school of thought (which is discussed in greater detail in 1 and is already well-known to readers and students of

Austrian Economics) comes to the conclusion that a sound monetary system is one in which money cannot "simply be printed out of thin air" as central banks have the power to do, but rather should be anchored to a valued commodity like gold. Proponents of sound money think that this stability provides the needed foundation for economic growth, while also reducing the likelihood of more significant societal problems such as war and poverty.

This was the situation with E-Gold, which was established in 1996 by Doug Jackson, who had previously worked as a physician. (Though not formally a cypherpunk, his case is nonetheless instructive, as it highlights an attempt to create a private gold-backed payments network). Because Jackson was so convinced that what he was doing was right, he gave up his lucrative oncology practice and started the company. E-Gold accounts were backed by audited warehouses of gold bullion, and on this foundation, an active digital payments network was developed. This network reached a milestone of more than one million members in the year 2004, and it continues to thrive today. However, in the end, the company would fail because of allegations that it did not comply with regulations governing money transmitters in the United States. As a result, all of the gold that was in the company's accounts would be essentially frozen pursuant to a plea agreement reached in July of 2008.

Satoshi provided a solution that he claimed would achieve a satisfactory amount of privacy as well as the monetary stability they needed, all within a technological framework that would extend the ability of bitcoin to function globally and beyond the authority of central authorities. He did this by appealing to both schools of thought. He stated that his method would fulfill these goals. In this post from 2009, at the era of initial deployment, he provided the following remark expressing this plea. He also cited cost of value transfer as a concern, which was handled in the that came before this one that dealt with technology: "The fundamental issue with traditional currency is that so much trust is necessary in order for it to function properly. The public must have faith that the central bank would not engage in currency debasement, despite the fact that the past of fiat currencies is replete with examples of broken public faith. However, despite being entrusted to retain our money and electronically transfer it, banks lend it out in waves of credit bubbles with hardly any of it kept in reserve. This violates the public trust. We are required to entrust them with our privacy and have faith that they will not allow identity thieves to empty our bank accounts. Their enormous operating expenses prevent them from accepting micropayments.

The Use Of Augmented Reality.

The practice of investigating the real environment by means of your device, such as a phone or camera, or directly is an example of augmented reality. The real world is transformed into a visual representation of the real world by adding computer-generated inputs such as still sounds, images, or movies to the real world. The primary distinction between augmented reality and virtual reality is that the former modifies the real world while the latter creates a whole new environment. It does not construct a whole new world from start for its users; rather, it merely adds to what is already present in the universe. The physical world and the digital world are unable to communicate with one another or even respond to one another in any way. However, the designer of augmented reality has designed it in such a way that it features a blended hybrid that is referred to as "mixed reality," which enables interaction to take place between the augmented digital world and the real world.

The various flavors of augmented reality

The accessibility of augmented reality is one of the technology's most remarkable features. It is not necessary to have extensive knowledge of the internet in order to participate in the realm of augmented reality. With the use of users' smartphones, the firms that developed augmented reality are making it possible for users to have fun while making use of augmented reality. Because of this, augmented reality is becoming increasingly popular.

The following are some examples of augmented reality:

AR based on markers

Marker-based augmented reality is also known as recognition-based augmented reality (AR) or image recognition. When you use this type of augmented reality, you are able to have access to additional information regarding a specific object that you are interested in learning more things about. Therefore, the augmented reality zeroes down on that object and provides the relevant information you require at that moment.

Based on markers One can utilize augmented reality in a variety of ways. It is able to identify the thing that is in front of your camera and can even display information regarding that object on your screen. Because a separate marker replaces the marker on the screen with a 3D depiction of the object that matches, the object can be recognized. This allows the user to examine the thing from a variety of perspectives while viewing more specific information about it. When you rotate your marker, the 3D picture will likewise rotate in sync with your movements.

The augmented reality that is based on superimposition.

The view of the thing that is now in focus can be replaced with an augmented reality overlay. This can be accomplished by substituting an item with an augmented view for either the entire or a portion of the view being altered.

The augmented reality that does not use markers

This form of augmented reality sees widespread application in the business world. Because so many modern smartphones are equipped with sensors that can determine a user's location, this type of augmented reality is also known as location-based augmented reality. When they are out on the road, the vast majority of users consult this kind of software for guidance. Additionally, it assists the user in looking for fascinating sites in the area that they are currently in. You may find out where the user is standing in addition to reading the data from the GPS, accelerometer, and digital compass on your mobile phone. For this augmented reality (AR) experience to work correctly, all you have to do is use the camera on your device to provide information about the location of an object on the screen.

That was the projection. The use of augmented reality.

The projection of light onto a specific surface constitutes this type of augmented reality, which is the simplest form of the technology. When light is presented on a surface, the projection-based augmented reality becomes interactive and engaging. Communication can take place by just touching the projected surface with your hand. The projected-based kind of augmented reality is mostly utilized for the purposes of creating the position, depth, and orientation of an item. Because of this, the user will be able to think about the many objects and the structure to study in greater detail. Try out this technology in order to generate virtual items that may be deployed over a larger area.

Investing Basics

Investing can be broken down into a great number of categories and subcategories. Spending money with the intention of making a profit from that spending is the most fundamental understanding of the term "investing" as it relates to one's own finances. One other name for this concept is "return on investment." A straightforward illustration of this strategy would be to purchase a house at one price, hold onto it for a few years, and then sell it at a higher price. Your profit is equal to the amount that the price at which you sold the home is higher than the price at which you purchased it. The concept of "investment" has also been used to different elements of our lives at various points in time. A good example of an investment in one's health would be to engage in activities that are beneficial to one's health. For the purposes of this book, we shall be concentrating on several types of financial investments.

Investing requires a significant commitment of time, mental toughness, physical effort, intellectual curiosity, and religious conviction. I say have faith because if you have done all of the necessary research and taken all of the necessary actions, then luck will play a significant role in the results. There is no way that random chance can be the deciding element. Especially when it comes to investments for the long run. At some time, skill is going to have to come into play as well.

Investing may be a difficult endeavor, particularly when one is just beginning out in the field. A large number of alternatives results in a large number of possible phrases, methods, and courses of action. Because of this, there are a lot of options to examine. No matter how much experience you have, making investments will never become simple. There will always be factors that are out of your hands, and there is no way to anticipate everything that could happen. The most effective strategy is to perform thorough study and to possess the attributes discussed earlier.

All of the strategies for changing one's perspective that we have gone over so far have been leading up to this point. Without these adjustments, we will never muster the bravery to make an investment. We have decided to take the easy route for the rest of our life and steer clear of as much trouble as we possibly can. It is a fact that the lower the level of risk that is taken, the lower the likelihood of a catastrophic failure occurring. You will, however, be forced to live a constrained life and will miss out on a wide variety of financial opportunities that are out there for you to take advantage of.

The more money you put into investments, the more you stand to lose. It is difficult to avoid this. You need to learn to be okay with the fact that you will not always be correct and accept that this is the case. You have to be willing to get up off the ground after falling on your face. The majority of people can't even fathom the possibility of having as much wealth as some of the most successful investors in history have lost. This occurred as a direct result of their willingness to take significant risks in order to maximize their potential rewards.

Warren Buffett, who is widely regarded as the undisputed maestro of stock market investment and who has amassed a fortune worth multiples of a billion dollars, is frequently recognized as one of the wealthiest men in the world. It is extremely difficult to forecast what his net worth will be by the time you finish reading this section because his wealth is subject to significant swings. In any event, the rankings will reveal how much they are currently worth, but they will not indicate how much value they have lost along the way. Over the course of his career, Warren Buffett has racked up billions in losses. He is still regarded as one of the most successful investors of all time, if not the most successful investor ever.

It is not our intention to make you into the next Warren Buffett with the help of this book. If this occurs for you, then you should feel congratulated. We merely wanted to demonstrate the mentality that one needs to adopt in order to become an investor. You can't let the possibility of failure get to you. You can't wallow in your failures; you have to focus instead on achieving as much success as possible. Regardless of the circumstances, you must always retain a positive attitude and a clear head.

When you are ready to start making investments, you have officially opened up your mind to all of the different kinds of money that are available. When you finally figure out how to get your hands on that huge pot of money that is out there, you will have the ability to build up a significant fortune for yourself. Knowledge of how the market functions is essential for a successful investing career. Since you are now prepared, we will walk you through the process of comprehending this as well.

Where to Begin and How to Do It

In order for you to become a successful stock investor, the following are the steps that you need to do.

Determine the level of risk you are willing to take – You need to determine your level of comfort with the various types of financial risk before you spend your hard-earned money on stock investments. Are you the type of person who enjoys taking chances? Are you in a position to risk some of your capital in the hope of realizing significant returns? Or do you like the option of investing your money in supposedly "safe" financial products such as savings accounts? What course of action would you take if, within a week, the value of your assets dropped by thirty percent? Will you liquidate all of your stocks or will you keep them?

Using these questions, you may evaluate whether or not you have the skills necessary to manage investments in stocks. You should keep in mind that the price of stocks can change rapidly, meaning that you could make or lose a significant amount of money in a relatively short length of time.

Taking a chance (Image courtesy of flickr.com)

Determine how much of your time and work you are willing to put into the project – In addition to the financial resources necessary, you will also need to invest time and effort into the management of your stock portfolio. Before you invest your money, you need to choose, investigate, and keep an eye on several companies. If you are unable to commit the necessary amount of time and effort into performing all of these things on a consistent basis, it is strongly recommended that you select an other kind of investment.

Diversifying your portfolio means spreading your investments over a number of different markets. Investing all of one's money in a single business or market is analogous to placing all of one's eggs in a single basket, and it is generally considered to be a poor financial strategy. This is due to the fact that if the firm or industry that you have chosen faces setbacks, then the entirety of your portfolio will suffer. On the other hand, if your capital is dispersed among a number of various industries, you will be shielded against rapid price reversals as well as losses in terms of your finances.

Make Your First Portfolio with These Easy Steps - Because you are just beginning to grasp how the stock market operates, there are several sectors and firms that you should steer clear of investing in. It is highly recommended that you base the construction of your investing portfolio on index funds, which are funds that are designed to replicate the performance of particular markets. According to those who specialize in finance, the most advantageous choices are funds that follow a broad market (such as the S&P 500) or small enterprises (such as the Russell 2000).

Construct a portfolio through the purchase of individual stocks Once you have acquired the necessary knowledge and expertise, you will be able to broaden your investment portfolio through the purchase of stocks from individual firms. Keep in mind that you need to broaden your investment horizons and diversify your portfolio. That means you need to buy shares from somewhere between 14 and 20 different companies. This range enables you to maintain a strong portfolio while minimizing the amount of companies that require your attention at any given time.

Begin to engage in investment activity – As soon as you feel comfortable with your ideas for investment, it is time to start purchasing stocks. Open a brokerage account by first finding a stock broker (beginners typically opt to do this online), then filling out the necessary paperwork, and finally depositing money into the account. It is recommended that you invest your money in a calm and steady manner. Even though you have carefully planned out your financial strategies, you still can't just throw all of your money away by taking unnecessary risks.

Increase the size of your stock holdings. As you gain more knowledge about the stock market, you will almost probably find that your choices about investments shift and evolve as a result. For instance, if you wish to increase the number of stocks you own in a different firm, you can decide to liquidate all of the shares you own in a particular company first. These adjustments are necessary to maintain the health of your portfolio and ensure that it continues to generate profits. However, you should try to limit these modifications as much as possible. According to those who specialize in finance, raising your financial capital is the most effective method for adjusting your portfolio. You will be able to increase your stock holdings and subsequently your profits if you proceed in this manner.

Instruments to Aid in Analysis

There is the scientific approach, there is the artistic approach, and then there are the tools that can assist you choose the correct companies to monitor and study. Screeners are one of these instruments, and they can take on a variety of shapes. The better ones will give you access to additional information pertinent to value investing, like cash on hand, cash flow, return on assets, and profitability, among other relevant metrics. Then there are some screeners that will merely show you how the company's stock price swings, which in most cases has absolutely nothing to do with the subject matter of this book. Certain screeners need payment in order to gain access or actual accounts. There are some of them that already come wrapped. Stock Rover, TradingView, and TC2000 are three examples of good trading platforms.

In addition to it, there are calculators and analyzers. The analyzers provide a breakdown of the company's present and future value based on certain assumptions, in addition to other financial information, while the calculators assist you in performing the necessary mathematical calculations in regard to the companies that you have selected.

If you want to be successful at value investing, you should learn as much as you can from those who came before you so that you can have an idea of the path you should take. This entails modeling one's actions after those of very successful people, such as Warren Buffet. It also means gaining access to information that will assist you in improving your decision-making skills and expanding your knowledge of value investing in general. There are annual fees associated with using some of these resources, but you will realize that the money spent was well worth it. You should subscribe to the "Hidden Gems" newsletters offered by Morningstar, Value Line, and The Motley Fool.

Invest Your Money Like A Pro!

The Professional Investor

The professional investor typically does not keep a close eye on their holdings on a daily basis. up point of fact, many only check up on their investments once every three months or once every six months. The reason for this is because the professional investor has created investments that are gradual and steady, paying interest at regular intervals, and are investments that are safe enough so that the investor does not have to worry about pulling out at the correct time. Many of these assets are on a massive scale, and because of this, wealthy people may get by on an annual interest rate of only three percent. Consider the operation of a trust fund as an example of a professional investor so that you may get a better handle on this concept.

A trust fund is a pool of money that is managed by seasoned investors who are tasked with earning a consistent return on assets that are considered to be low risk. Because maximizing returns is not how a professional investor thinks about their job, a trust fund does not have that goal in mind. They are more concerned with trying to increase their wealth while staying within a predetermined level of danger. The fact that they are able to generate consistent profits is the single most essential consideration. The pool of money that they are dealing with and the regulations that govern how this money is to be distributed are what enable them to make investments that are so cautious. A trust is able to function because a significant quantity of money is placed in a fund that is then used for investment purposes. The trustees are only given the interest that has been accrued on the fund. There are certain exceptions, and trusts can be established in a number of various ways, but if you've seen a trust that's been around for a hundred years, for example one that funds scholarships, then this is a trust that only finances its trustees through the accrual of interest. When examining the endowment of a university, it is easy to see how a return of one percent on one billion dollars might become rather significant. Ten million dollars, or one percent of one billion dollars, is hardly a negligible amount of money by any stretch of the imagination. Although it may be more difficult for us to replicate these types of assets on a scale that is appropriate for our level of investment, this does not imply that we do not have access to trusts or investments that are considered to be safe.

It is possible for us to have the same types of assets as the extremely wealthy, and I strongly recommend that you keep at least one of the following investment opportunities in mind while making decisions. Because they are investments, you will need to continue contributing money to them, and the interest that you earn will continue to increase with each dollar that you contribute. Although it is possible that you would never get as much as a billion dollars from your first investment, the more money you put in, the higher your returns will be. For my own part, each and every return on investment is placed in this particular account. I take the money that I generate from my other investments and divide it up so that I may put it in two of the three funds that are listed below (you will soon understand why I don't invest in just one fund). My returns in the distant future will increase in proportion to the growth of each fund. These funds, in addition to being exceptionally risk-free, can provide significant financial benefits in the form of reduced taxable income and capital gains. It will be made evident in the following that taxes on these investments made for the long term are levied at a far more advantageous rate than taxes on investments made for the short term.

I ran out of energy but was confident that I had found my calling, so I leapt into my truck.

I had just recently left a steakhouse where I had just finished giving a talk to around thirty doctors about various topics including medication, cash, and land. The majority of them had kept my group and myself there, asking questions for two hours after the event had ended, which is the reason why I was so worn out.

Why would thirty busy professionals want to take time out of their schedules on a Monday evening to listen to somebody talk about opportunities and money? They were there due to the reality that, in today's world, physicians are forced to choose between a vocation that they adore and a business that they despise. Those who were eating supper together were looking for answers to address the division that existed. They had an insatiable appetite for learning and were searching for answers to help them lead a happier and healthier lifestyle. I had stumbled across my calling.

— — — — — — —

Today's medical professionals are torn between a vocation that they adore and

a business that they despise. — — — —
— — —

You have to understand that we were never taught to pursue wealth when we were in medical school. We were taught to view ourselves as "poor." Permit me to elaborate. The helpless specialists spend everything they earn, and because they don't have to worry about their standard of living, they are able to labor nonstop. Their unquestionable level of education was not designed to make them wealthy; rather, its purpose was to educate them to the point where they could become professionals in their fields.

Even though the vast majority of the people in that room were most likely exceptionally talented doctors (and may have been in possession of enormous ledgers), the world of genuinely creating abundance was foreign to them. They had not yet mastered the ability to think like "rich specialists," or professionals who have mastered the art of making their ability to bring in money work for them. A wealthy expert is one who is financially educated, values the possibility for choice, and moves through life with reason, energy, and management. This assembly required that opportunity, and don't you think all of us do, too?

As a result, we utilized the extra time in the late evening to respond to concerns regarding control and generate straightforward money. There were comments like "I didn't realize you could do that!" and more like them. or "I didn't realize how trapped I was until I heard you speak." The energy was really electrifying! This group of people made enough money to pay their bills, but they were confused and wanted a genuine balance between things that were fun and activities that were serious. The public perception of experts as wealthy ignores the fact that the individual costs associated with maintaining that status are adversely affecting both the specialists and the patients they treat.

Exactly What Does It Mean To Be Considered "Rich"?

Before we get into some of the steps you'll need to take on your journey to riches, it's important to have a solid understanding of what it means to be considered "rich."

It doesn't matter if you call it being financially independent, independently affluent, or anything else; at its core, being rich implies having an excess of money or assets, sufficient to live your life the way you choose to spend it.

You are considered affluent if you have enough money or assets to live your life according to the parameters that you choose for yourself, despite the fact that we all have our own unique ideas about how we would like to spend our lives.

For some people, this may mean quitting their job or career in order to pursue a passion or launch their own business. Some individuals might not be able to work at all. On the other side, some people may want to keep working so that they can afford a more extravagant way of life.

Therefore, the specific amount of money that is connected with the word wealthy might vary, but the overriding principle is that you have the ability to live your life however you desire because you have the finances or assets to support that lifestyle.

The First Eight Steps to Your Financial Success

The majority of affluent people achieved their level of wealth by adhering to a rather straightforward plan over a significant amount of time in order to get there, with the notable exception being bitcoin billionaires and people like Jeff Bezos.

If you do what I say and follow these steps, you'll put yourself in a good position to become wealthy as well.

1. Commit to making it a priority.

You need, above all else, to set a priority on elevating your financial situation.

Studies have shown that those who deliberately set goals for themselves are up to ten times more likely to succeed in accomplishing those goals.

Simply focusing on "getting rich" as your objective won't cut it. In order for you to maintain your concentration on the target, it is important that you make your objective as specific and attainable as possible.

What connotations does the word "rich" evoke in your mind? Do you have aspirations of accumulating a million-dollar fortune? A million dollars put out of pocket? Will one million be sufficient, or do you require more, or possibly even fewer?

Calculating your financial independence number (also known as your FI number) is a more accurate method for determining how much money you will require in the future. While it is OK to use an arbitrary number to represent wealth, doing so can be time-consuming. Your financial independence number is the sum of money you'll require to be able to continue living the way you do now without having to earn a living for the rest of your life.

Even though you can get a ballpark figure by multiplying your annual expenses by 25 (representing the number of years you plan to spend in "retirement"), it is essential to take into account factors such as inflation, withdrawal rate, and investment growth.

It is imperative that those who are thinking about adopting the FIRE (financial independence, retire early) lifestyle perform a more in-depth calculation of their FI number in order to ensure that they have everything they require.

It is important to make an estimate of how much money or assets you'll need to attain your goal of getting wealthy, so that you have something concrete to strive for and can plan around it. This can be done regardless of the approach that you ultimately decide to take.

Put on Your Snorkel Before You Dive Is the Topic of the Third Section of Six

Don't Shorten Your Own Life Expectancy by Doing This!

If you read this book and take away nothing else, let it be this: there is no endeavor that is worthwhile enough to warrant jeopardizing your mental health. You may come across the most lucrative real estate investment deal available, the deal of the century, but if the pursuit of that deal would cause you to experience disturbed sleep at night or other times of the day, it is not a good idea. To me, life is not about tallying up the numbers. As far as I'm concerned, happiness is the objective of life, and there is no monetary value that can be put on contentment. I don't think it's possible to buy contentment. This also has implications for life beyond the land. There are such a great number of options available to you in life for you to give up some portion of your mental wellbeing in exchange for something.

As was mentioned earlier, one of the major advantages of investing in real estate is that there are a wide variety of options available for how the investment can be carried out. As a result, you can almost surely find a strategy that allows you to put money in your pocket while also allowing you to relax in the evenings. You have the ability to choose what helps you remain rational in addition to what makes you happy as a result of the abundance of options. This is not to imply that there won't ever be pressure involved with whichever land contributing course you choose; however, there should be a hidden fulfillment and facilitate that keeps you traveling through those anxieties, as if there isn't, it will be extremely simple and enticing to give up. This is because if there isn't, it will be extremely easy and tempting to give up.

My approach to selecting a strategy for making financial speculations is to prioritize those that make use of the natural qualities I possess. Have you ever heard of 'reinforcing your qualities' rather than 'fortifying your shortcomings'? If so, when did you first learn about this concept? What happens in the event that we are willing to work on improving our strengths rather than seeking to improve our weaknesses?

Imagine a well-organized presentation that analyzes your skills and qualities, highlighting the aspects in which you excel and highlighting the areas in which you are deficient.

I have created one specifically for myself:

The higher you set the standard, the more confident I feel in my proficiency in that area. The lower you set the standard, the more vulnerable I become.

If I were to follow the old tradition says I should try to reinforce my weaknesses by raising the low bars, I would do the opposite of what the legend says I should do. In order to demonstrate my point, I will ignore the instruction to "work like a typical person out on the town" because I am not even sure how to respond to that specific instruction. Consequently, let's assume that in order to become more grounded in those areas, I will focus on go-go dancing, learning how to cook, and figuring out how to fill out the necessary paperwork for the government. I am taking cooking classes, dance classes, and responsibility courses in order to (attempt to) strengthen those areas in which I am lacking. Let's take a look at a chart that lays down the progress I've made in each of those categories:

You will be able to observe on the diagram the extent to which I had the opportunity to improve upon such capabilities by making an effort to fortify them. The go-go out was the part that required the most preparation due to the fact that I desperately desired to learn how to do the go-go dance.[6] Cooking was something I worked on for a while, but since I didn't particularly enjoy it, I let it slide up until this point. Also, evaluation forms... yes, I actually fell asleep while attempting.

In two of the three talents, I made an effort to go away from what I was trying to do. Have you ever noticed how it's not exactly typical to enjoy doing things that you are terrible at? I might keep trying to learn go-go out, and I might even like the process of trying to learn it, but the fact that go-go out isn't one of my normal attributes won't ever change. Even walking around in high heels is difficult for me, so the thought of dancing in them is laughable.

Now that you've seen the information following me attempting to cope with my deficiencies, how about we take a look at how I did when I attempted to attempt to work on my regular qualities of mathematics, piloting an airplane, and line movement instead:

Compare the number of additional opportunities I had to bolster my strengths with the number of additional opportunities I had to bolster my weaknesses. Look at the difference. In most cases, these are hypothetical scenarios, but the reasoning behind them is based on the observation that we as a whole are most successful at activities that we are naturally good at and that we enjoy doing. In addition, isn't it true that we tend to value things more when we have a firm grasp on how to use them effectively? Take note of this virtuous cycle: the more we excel at something, the greater our appreciation for it, and the more our appreciation for it, the more we excel at it. In addition, rather commonly, both of these things, namely happiness and the capability to dominate, are connected with the innate ability sets that we each possess.

I didn't just make up how this works; it's based on legitimate scientific research.

CliftonStrengths[7] is a remarkable resource that can be utilized to learn more about this topic.

When I say "go with your regular grain," I'm referring to this particular thing. It's not out of the ordinary for people to point out our inadequacies to us, but the question is: why should we try to improve them? Since it is unlikely that any one of us will be exceptional at everything that life throws at us, why not focus on the things that we are naturally predisposed toward and that bring us the most joy?

It is beneficial to occasionally step outside of your normal comfort zone and make an effort to improve in areas that are less familiar to you. Doing so can be quite rewarding. I totally support you doing that, but I don't really endorse you doing that in an effort to transform yourself into somebody else when you're not already that person. If everything else stays the same, you should perform the action as an afterthought or when you have enough spare time (or money) to do it for fun.

As a land investor, it goes without saying that the majority of my regular grain is in investment properties. I am familiar with the process, and I have generally been able to readily excel at managing investment homes. Taking care of investment properties has been something that has come naturally to me throughout my life. Would I have gone with the purchase of investment properties as my preferred choice of speculative investment? Not at all; I probably would have gone with flipping. The idea that I could make a lot of money in a relatively short amount of time by flipping houses is intriguing, and even if I didn't make a lot of money doing it, I think it would be fun. On the other hand, in the event that you observed me attempt to negotiate a sale or deal with a worker for hire, you would recognize that flipping isn't vital for the typical fiber of my business. Because I have a tendency to be so naive with construction workers, I currently have in my home what are likely the most expensive shelves in the world. This is not due to the fact that they are particularly luxurious racks. Consequently, despite the fact that, on the surface level, choosing to flip real estate sounds like it would be the most lucrative choice I could make regarding a strategy for land speculation, the reality is that it is in no way, shape, or form the best choice for me.

When it comes to investment properties, on the other hand, I can easily move that bar up without any problems at all. I have the capability of learning how to flip, but despite the fact that the whole concept of flipping seems exciting, the skills that are required for flipping make me feel as though I will never be able to do it. In addition to this, the talents are so alien to me that it's quite possible that I'll be able to train myself to be really good at it. This is not to suggest that I should never flip a property, as I do believe that it has the potential to be a wonderful side endeavor and that it may provide me with some helpful information; but, for me, it should be primarily that—a pleasurable side venture rather than one that I am depending on for money. When I'm dependent on something for money, I really want an option that I can move all the more quickly with and doesn't require me to take on an excessive lot of risk by doing something I'm not very good at.

After revealing my inner-reference-diagram-obsessed self, I'm going to assume that you understand what I mean when I recommend focusing on the things that come to you the most naturally. There are a lot of reasons why one should not shift their focus from those things.

It is not difficult to begin searching out for things that work out well for you, even if you do not currently have a concept of what works out easily for you; in fact, the majority of us do not. To begin, you should experiment with the many options available inside land contributing. Attend lectures, make time to read, and study in a classroom setting. You don't need to spend every last dime on this, but the first step in figuring out what comes to you more easily is to educate yourself about the various options that are there. During this time, you'll notice that you start to have a preference for certain freedoms over others. This preference will become more pronounced as time goes on.

The Building Blocks Of Day Trading

You can follow the standard procedures while investing in equities. Therefore, you have the option of purchasing mutual funds or paying a stockbroker to handle your portfolio on your behalf. On the other hand, taking this path will only take you so far. You are going to be rather astonished to see that the prospective profits are not particularly impressive.

Many people who invest decide to do so on their own since the returns they receive are not particularly impressive. This is the motivation behind their decision to engage in day trading. In the following section, we will discuss the foundations of day trading, as well as the reasons why you might find it to be a beneficial decision for you.

The Meaning of the Term "Day Trading"

Day trading is a method of stock investment in which the investor retains complete discretion over the management of their portfolio. In other words, it is up to the investor to choose which stocks to purchase and which to sell. Additionally, the investor is the one who decides the timing of the trades.

Day trading is an example of a trading strategy that focuses on the short term. The same trading day is used for opening and closing positions by investors. As a result, individuals are able to begin and end each day with a fresh slate. The rationale for this is that it is more straightforward. If you leave positions alone overnight, you expose yourself to the possibility of being affected by elements from the outside. As a consequence, there is a possibility of sudden changes in price action.

As a result, investors try to protect themselves against potential losses by liquidating all of their positions before the market closes for the day. As a result, they call it a day and pay out. When investors take this method, they are able to avoid having to deal with any potential price shocks that may come at the beginning of the trading day. This is a very practical strategy.

Day trading is an excellent option for novice traders who have a limited amount of capital to deposit but are interested in generating profits in the short term. Day trading could be a component of a broader investing strategy for those who have access to bigger amounts of funds for investment purposes.

Day Trading: Where to Start and How to Get Started

Day trading requires that you have a brokerage account in order to get started. An agreement that you enter into with a financial institution is what is known as a brokerage account. This organization holds all necessary licenses to conduct business in the stock market. Consequently, this business organization grants you permission to use their trading platform in order to participate in the market. In a nutshell, you start acting as your own stockbroker. The fact that you are totally liable for whatever that takes place is the one and only drawback. Therefore, if you blow through all of your cash, you have no one else but yourself to blame but yourself.

There are primarily two kind of brokerage accounts to choose from. One type of account is known as a "full service" account. This type of account provides you with all of the bells and whistles available. These accounts impose a cost for opening the account in addition to charging transaction fees for each individual trade. Despite this, they give you access to real-time quotations as well as analytics. In addition to this, they offer professional guidance and suggestions. In this way, they make it easier for you to decide how to distribute your financial resources.

A "discount" account is the other category of account that can be held. When you open an account with a discount broker, the primary benefit you will obtain is access to the trading platform; however, you will not have access to additional features. As a result, you need to figure out where you can obtain information on the stocks that you want to trade in order to fulfill this need. The fact that discount brokers just require a one-time sign-up cost is one of the advantages they offer. Additionally, the transaction costs that are charged for each trade are reduced. On the other hand, rather of opting for a pay-as-you-go strategy, you will be required to purchase trading bundles.

You are able to begin trading immediately after opening a brokerage account in your name. It is not too difficult to accomplish. However, keep in mind that the terms and conditions of different brokerage accounts can vary. If you want to participate in some, you may need to have an investment capital of several thousand dollars, while others may demand you to have as little as five hundred dollars.

Remember to take advantage of the free demo account; this is a very crucial part of the process. A demo account will provide you with cost-free access to the trading platform offered by any respectable brokerage service. Demo accounts allow players to experience the full version of the game but with play money instead of real cash. You are trading on the real platform, using real data and analytics, but you are not trading with real money. This is one of the many reasons why a demo account is so useful. It gives you the opportunity to practice your trading technique before you put it into action with real money. It enables you to learn from your mistakes without running the risk of completely ruining your financial situation.

4 Automated Investment Strategies That Require No Research

I get it; you might not have the time to research companies or you might not feel like doing so since it doesn't pique your interest. Fortunately, there is a way to continue investing even when the research has already been done by others; all you need to do is have recurrent investment turned on and continue to invest. I get it. The following topics will be covered:

Index and Exchange-Traded Funds

AKA: "mutual funds"

Investments in Hedge Funds

The rise of the robot advisors

ETFs and Index Funds: A portfolio of stocks or bonds that attempts to imitate the performance of the broader financial markets is known as an index fund. Index funds are considered to be low-risk investments due to the fact that the underlying firms are forecasted to experience growth and investors are given a stake in all of the companies. The specialists who manage the portfolios make adjustments to the holdings so that they remain in line with market indices such as the Dow Jones, the S&P 500, and the Nasdaq. The three most important indexes are as follows.

Plan of action

The plan of action is not overly complicated. You should have an index fund in each of the three primary ones, as was discussed earlier, and you should distribute your investment budget across these ETFs so that it is equal. Because it is not possible to purchase index funds directly, investment professionals have developed ETFs that track the indexes instead. You will be able to passively prepare your portfolio for retirement while also diversifying it, but there will be annual costs that you will be required to pay. These fees are not very high. Yes, that's all there is to it; all you need to do is make deposits, and compound interest will do the rest of the work for you.

$QQQ, which tracks the Nasdaq, has annual costs of 0.20%, while $SPY, which tracks the S&P 500, has annual fees of 0.0945%, and $DIA, which tracks the Dow Jones, has annual fees of 0.16%.

The fact that each fund provides dividends in addition to a diversified portfolio is the best thing about it. Therefore, you will be engaging in passive investment and will be able to achieve passive income.

$QQQ on the Nasdaq has a dividend yield of 0.49%.

$SPY represents the S&P 500 and has a dividend yield of 1.3%.

$DIA represents a dividend yield of 1.61% for the Dow Jones.

The dividend payments, on their own, cover the cost of the index subscription, leaving you with additional funds that can be reinvested or set aside. You are receiving compensation for the work of financial experts who are building a portfolio on your behalf; what more could you ask for?

Interest that is Compounded

The performance of SPY over the past decade has resulted in a compound annual return of 16.51 percent. Over the past quarter century, a compound yearly return of 9.55 percent has been achieved. It is therefore reasonable to estimate that SPY provides a return of approximately 10 percent every year.

Suppose that...

Investing $500 each month between the ages of 22 and 65 yields an average annual return of 10%.

You will be able to retire with $3,555,000, and if you elect to put it to your 401(k) or Roth IRA, then none of it will be subject to taxation when you do so. You were able to accomplish this feat at a young age solely through the practice of investing in a passive manner. Since compound interest requires a period of time, it is in your best benefit to start investing as soon as possible.

Putting together a backup plan.

I first became interested in reading books about business when I was a senior in high school. (In most situations, I was good at getting things ready.) I studied some books about contributing to financial exchanges and others about land. When compared, land gained results in loss of control. It was unquestionably a useful resource that I was able to manage. To me, it seems like a horrible idea to put resources into the financial exchange. During my first year of dentistry school at Baylor College of Dentistry in Dallas (1980), I persuaded my father to be my co-adventure accomplice in getting a two-story block investment property (a domain deal) in a strong Dallas region. I did this while I was in the middle of my first year of dental school. We followed the first rule of real estate, which was to purchase the property in a desirable neighborhood that was noticeably the worst one there. I worked out how to take care of this primary source of income for the rental payment. Following our graduation from Baylor University in 1983, we decided to sell the house and divide the approximately $50,000.00 in capital increases benefit that we received. In contrast to normal or dynamic pay, the rate of charge for capital adds is significantly lower. The realization that I had created a capital gain of $25,000.00 from this one land resource during the very same timeframe that I worked many, multiple hours as a waiter during evening time and on ends of the week with far less to show for it in total remuneration was the revelation for me. When I could invest in wonderful financial resources that would work for me regardless of whether or not I worked, why would it be a good idea for me to spend the rest of my life working for money? I gradually came to understand that if I was able to accumulate sufficient riches, I wouldn't have to work as hard, if at all. Perhaps I wouldn't even have to work at all.

My "Plan B" consisted of purchasing land and investing my money in it so that I could transition away from working for money and toward investing my money in capital resources that would generate income, allow me to save money, and ultimately build wealth. Developing a backup strategy was the key to achieving financial freedom and escaping the 9-to-5 rat race. It was available whenever I wanted or required it the most. In 2004, while Jenna was being treated at the medical facility, I made the decision to pull the trigger. Given the foundation that enabled me to leave up my rewarding but financially demanding occupation as a dental specialist, I had to put in a lot of hard work, perform some acts of penance, and learn how to properly invest in real estate. It was not a straightforward decision, but rather one for which I had a genuine "reason why."

Both the Markets and the Brokers

There are several sub-categories of financial markets to choose from. You will need to place most of your focus on the stock market if you want to make investments; the reason for this will become clear to you once I describe the many types of instruments that are available. Both the Securities and Exchange Commission (SEC) and the Financial Regulatory Authority (FINRA) are responsible for overseeing the stock market's regulatory processes. The primary focus of the SEC is on market activities, whereas the FINRA is responsible for regulating market institutions.

In spite of all of the bad commentary that surrounds these establishments, the reality is that when compared to other countries' marketplaces, those in the United States are the most open and well-regulated. You could, for instance, try investing in the Chinese stock market and see if you can make any sense of it or whether you have any legal options available to you in the event that something goes wrong.

The existence of hedge funds in the market and the purported way in which they tilt the scales against individual investors are topics that are frequently discussed on social media. It's true that hedge funds have advantages in execution and infrastructure compared to small investors, but the idea that hedge funds purposefully target mom-and-pop investors to take their money is ridiculous.

It is comparable to the New York Yankees trying their best to devise a game plan and win against a high school baseball club. The Yankees won't even be aware of the existence of that minor league squad for the most part. The primary goal of hedge funds is to generate profits for its investors. Because pension funds are one of the hedge fund industry's largest clients, a surprising number of investors choose to invest only a very small amount of money.

Putting hedge funds to the side for a while, it is imperative that you let go of the idea that someone is trying to take advantage of you in the markets. This is a constrained attitude that will cause you to notice unfavorable aspects in everything, and it is challenging to generate income when you have such a mindset. Instead, you should realize that the majority of investors are not overly concerned with factors that they cannot control or fully comprehend. In the following , which is dedicated to teaching you sound investment principles, I will go into further detail on this topic.

For the time being, let's take a more in-depth look at the various financial instruments into which you might invest your money.

Musical Apparatus

Stocks are the most often used instruments since they are the most easily accessible and transparent financial product. The Securities and Exchange Commission (SEC) is in charge of regulating the stock market and establishing laws that all publicly traded corporations are required to follow. Every publicly traded company is required to publish annual and quarterly financial reports, which are made available without charge to shareholders and other market participants.

In addition to these forms, firms are required to make a whole host of other filings in order to retain their legal standing. Examples of these filings include information regarding insider trading and changes in ownership. For instance, if a director of the company sells their shares, this transaction is documented and reported with the SEC (Palmer, 2019). Similarly, if an employee sells their shares, this information is also recorded and filed.

It seems to reason that a stock's long-term price forecast will be reflective of a company's performance given that a share of stock implies direct ownership of a portion of a corporation. On the other hand, in the short run, stock prices might be affected by speculative excitement. There are a lot of speculators that try to time when they enter the market, which ends up pushing prices in a certain direction. This does not imply that stock prices are artificially influenced; rather, it indicates that speculators have a tendency to mimic one another and ultimately end up pushing prices in the direction that they prefer. If you want to make money off of stock investments, you should plan to hold on to your holdings for the long term, which is defined as more than ten years.

Bonds are the second most common financial instrument, and similar to stocks, they can be used for either speculative or investing purposes. A bondholder is a creditor of a firm and is entitled to receive interest payments according to a predetermined schedule. The price of the bond will drop if the corporation fails to make its payment, which will attract investors who speculate on financial outcomes.

Ratings organizations assess the potential profitability of an investment in each and every bond. If they have an investment rating, this does not mean that they are guaranteed to be risk-free, but it does mean that the possibility of them defaulting on their obligations is low. Bonds are an option for investment, but they are typically pricey and need considerable sums of money to purchase. Because of this, the majority of investors opt to keep their money in equities.

You are able to purchase derivatives on the stock market in addition to traditional investments such as stocks and bonds. Instruments such as options and futures can be considered derivatives since they are tied to another instrument and "derive" their value from that instrument. Although there is absolutely no method to invest in them, a large number of individual investors have placed their money in them (Graham, 1998).

To begin, these derivatives have a finite lifespan and typically become worthless within a month; even the derivatives with the longest lifespans only remain valid for a maximum of one year. Call options, also known as derivatives, are becoming increasingly popular as a result of unethical brokers' efforts to sell them to regular investors in order to increase their commissions. Call options give you the right to buy a stock at a specified price. On the other hand, this does not imply that investing in calls is something you should do. To avoid making mistakes, it's best to steer clear of derivatives wherever possible.

Many people are interested in commodities like gold, silver, and oil because of their value. To tell you the truth, every commodity is unique and behaves differently in accordance with its own economic cycle of supply and demand. It is not recommended to put one's money into anything other than gold or silver as a long-term investment. This is due to the fact that despite the fact that they are more speculative in nature, due to their popularity, they are a feasible alternative. This is in contrast to silver, which is an asset due to the fact that it has usefulness. Later on in this book, I'll describe how you might put together a portfolio that includes these different types of instruments.

Last but not least, we have foreign exchange, sometimes known as purely speculative currencies. It is difficult to fathom how foreign exchange (FX) instruments could ever be considered an asset because they are essentially just reflections of the exchange rate that exists between two currencies.

An Introduction To Investing In Stocks For Novices

The answer to this question will change depending on the perspective you take. People who are new to the world of long-term investing would be wise to consider stocks as an excellent long-term investment strategy. You are, on the other hand, mistaken if you believe that you can get quick cash from stock. The stock market is not a strategy for making rapid money. There are some things that are known to make you money in the long run, but not as quickly as some people think they will. One example of this is the tick. You should be aware that there are risks associated with investing in the stock market, and that this is the reason why you could not get wealthy as quickly as you had anticipated. If you want to make money from stocks, it is strongly recommended that you do not invest all of your money in a single business. Purchase stock in a variety of firms because you believe they have room for expansion.

To be successful in making money from the financial market, extensive planning is required. You will need to determine which stocks you want to purchase as well as the company from which you want to purchase the "hare." Before you begin purchasing any of them, you need to do some research on the various companies and stocks that are currently on the market.

Several Varieties of Stocks

You need to have an understanding of the many types of stocks that are available on the market nowadays;

Shares of Common Stock

This is the stock that is traded the most frequently on the market. The common stock typically grants you, the shareholder, the right to vote in each shareholder meeting that is conducted by the company; however, the number of votes you are granted is proportional to the number of shares you own in the company. Purchasing this kind of stock provides you, the shareholder, with enormous gains; nevertheless, it is a very risky investment since if the company goes bankrupt, you will have a good possibility of losing the money you invested in it. The common stock typically has dividends available, however these dividends might vary and are not always guaranteed. These shares can be purchased and sold using the company's ticker symbol.

Preferred Stock and Penny Stock are both types of Stock.

As opposed to common "tock," "preferred" "tock" signify a degree of ownership but do not come with any voting rights. This is in contrast to the "common" "tock," which do. The "tock," on the other hand, provides the investor with significant benefits, including the guarantee that they will always be paid a certain dividend. If you purchased preferred stock, you will receive payment first in the event of liquidation, ahead of those who purchased common stock. The ability of the firm to buy back its own shares at any time is one of the primary distinctions between common stocks and preferred stocks. Investors often believe that penny stocks provide an opportunity for significant returns on their investments. The stocks are also referred to as cent 'tocks' in some circles. These "tocks" are considered to

105

be "common stocks" for the "mall public company." Normal trading activity for the penny stock occurs at $5 or less.

The Various Categories That Are Employed

Before you can invest your money in the market, you need to make it a priority to gain an understanding of the various categories that firms use to put their stocks. If you do not have this knowledge, you will not be able to invest.

There is also a category called size, which refers to the total market capitalization. The market capitalisation of a company is typically calculated by multiplying the price per share by the total number of shares still outstanding. The companies that typically have a market capitalization of tens of billions of dollars are those that are classified as large by size. Large-cap firms are those that have what are known as "table stocks," and they are distinguished by this characteristic.

The style category is one that I have subdivided into two distinct subcategories: growth and value. A company that is expanding at a rate that is significantly faster than the industry average would typically issue growth stock. If you want to invest in the stock market, you should purchase the shares from a young age so that you can benefit from their subsequent growth. The e-tock is a risky investment since its value increases when the market is performing well but decreases when the market is performing poorly. On the other hand, the value of 'tock' increases in a methodical and consistent manner. These stocks trade at a rate that is lower than the industry standard.

The final category is denoted by the symbol ector. The "tock" are arranged into groups according to the many industries.

An Introduction To The World Wide Web Of Financial Transactions

1.1. The Ways in Which Technologies Are Changing the World

Good evening to each and every one of you! To be in this location brings me tremendous happiness. I've never been to Sweden before, so I'm trying to soak up as much of the country as possible—with the exception of the climate, of course. But other than that, everything is wonderful!

Since I still remember the very first time I attended a meeting related to the web, I must say that it is a very exciting experience to be here. That was in the year 1992. present were perhaps one hundred people present, and everyone there was either a computer researcher or an undergraduate student studying software engineering. Nobody believed us, despite the fact that we were assuring everyone that everything in the entire world was going to change. At the very least, nobody accepted me since I was 19 years old, off-kilter, and timid. Nobody believed us. But if there's one thing I took up from that experience, it's that I should always trust my gut instincts. Since, to tell you the truth, the internet altered how the world works.

The title of the second book series I've written is "The Internet of Money." The reasoning behind this is based on the premise that the innovation that I will talk about today is going to alter the globe in a comparable manner. In addition to that, it will alter the web itself.

1.1.1. Brand New Inventions, Age-Old Stories 1.1.1.

Bitcoin is a new financial innovation that was released on January 3, 2009 by an unknown creator. It was made available to the public as an open-source project, was worked on by volunteers from the surrounding community, and was managed as a distributed organization.

After then, it was laughed at, ignored, and discarded for the first five or six years after it was introduced. But not nearly as much as before.

People are beginning to zero in on specifics, just like they do with the internet. Things that were previously inexplicable are now within our grasp and can be accomplished. People are beginning to understand that this is the kind of thing that is more important than whatever it is that they are told. And what information do they receive? They have been informed that only cast offs make use of the facility. Pharmacists on the street! You're all pornographers! You scoundrels!

What do you think? In the first meeting ever held about the web, which took place in 1992, this was one of the things that was discussed. They were incorrect back then, and they continue to be incorrect now. This absurd story is undermined every time you come across an individual, such as a dental specialist or a beautician, who uses bitcoin as a form of payment.

Bitcoin is a convention, and there is no other forum more appropriate than this one to talk about a protocol.

1.2. What Does Money Represent?

The moment you start talking about Bitcoin and thinking about Bitcoin, a very difficult question is raised: what is cash? The vast majority of us are completely ignorant regarding the nature of cash and how it operates. It's one of those innovations that has become so deeply ingrained in our way of life that we no longer even notice it's there. It's one of those things that we take for granted. In point of fact, we don't have to give any thought to cash unless it suddenly stops operating. In some countries, paper money is rendered useless. And after that, everyone has fascinating views regarding the nature of monetary currency.

What exactly is cash? At the most fundamental level possible, money does not represent value. In point of fact, we use currency to purchase things that have significant worth (products or services), despite the fact that there is no value in the paper notes or coins themselves. In spite of the widespread misconception prevalent in today's society, money is not a source of power. This is despite the fact that all of our money coming from certain authorized sources. If a person wearing a crown tells you that "this is your money," then the statement has great weight. That is the source of the strength it possesses.

But what if there was no need for a central body to issue new currency? What if there was a way to generate new money simply by spending it? It has come to light that the true nature of money is that of a language. Money is a language that humans established in order to communicate to one another their respective values. It is one of the primary constructions of civilization, and as a language, it enables us to surpass a number that is called the Dunbar number. The maximum number of persons who can successfully contribute to the operation of a clan is known as the Dunbar number. In the event that you require the assistance of two clans, you should strive to attain the standard level of safety. These securities have included culture, language, religious beliefs, and monetary systems; these securities are an essential component of the development that has enabled humans to expand beyond the limits of a single clan and engage in trade and commerce with others on a more extensive scale.

Unexpectedly, control can also be exercised through the use of monetary systems. Those that are able to keep their hands on the cash have a tremendous advantage over others. In light of this, lords and state-run administrations have maintained a stringent command over monetary matters, just as they formerly maintained a stringent command over religious matters, and for the same set of reasons.

Covered Calls are discussed in detail in 16.

What Exactly Is Meant by a Covered Call?

The act of selling the right to purchase a specified asset that you hold at a given price within a specified amount of time, which is often shorter than one year, is described by this term, which is also known as a buy-write. In this transaction, the asset that is being sold is the right to purchase the asset at the specified price. It is a two-step technique in which an individual first buys stock and then sells it on the basis on the individual share values.

The profit that accrues to the seller in the form of a premium payment from the options holder is one of the many appealing aspects of this particular kind of option. Because the seller already owns the shares, there is less of a chance of something going wrong. Therefore, your expenses will be paid if there is a rise in the stock price that is more than the strike price. In the event that the trader decides to exercise the right to purchase on or before the expiration date, all you have to do is deliver as agreed and take advantage of any additional benefits.

The most typical underlying asset for a contract of this kind is a share of stock.

If you want to use covered calls, you have to be willing to own the stock at your price even if it goes down in price. Otherwise, you won't be able to use covered calls. Due to the volatility of the financial markets, it is important to keep in mind that there is no assurance that you will make a significant profit from the stock that you have purchased. As a result, you need to put in a lot of effort to maintain your concentration on finding high-quality stocks that you are willing to acquire. In the event that the market experiences a decline for an extended period of time, you need to be able to continue to have the potential to benefit from that ownership.

If you are going to sell covered call options, you need to be sure that you are willing to sell the underlying stock if the price goes up. If you have already signed into an option contract with a willing buyer, then you will not be able to alter your mind even if the price of the stock goes up. If the trader decides to exercise that option, you are obligated to carry out the delivery in question.

If the underlying stock price is at or above the call's strike price at or before the option's expiration date, then the covered call strategy has generated the greatest potential profit it is capable of producing. The solution to this problem can be expressed as follows:

The maximum potential profit is equal to the sum of the call premium plus the difference between the strike price and the stock price.

In addition to this, the vendor should think about the moment at which they will have broken even when the time limit has passed. The solution to this problem can be expressed as follows:

Break-even analysis is calculated by subtracting the call premium from the stock's purchase price.

Additionally, the seller is responsible for determining the highest potential risk. This is equivalent to the price at which the stock can be purchased while maintaining a break-even point.

Additionally, the seller must be content with both the stocks' static rate of return and their if-called rate of return before the sale can go through. The static return is the approximate annual net profit that may be made from a covered call. This is calculated under the assumption that there will be no change in the price of the underlying stock either before or after the option's expiration date. In order for the vendor to arrive at this value, they need to know:

The cost of purchasing that particular share of stock

The price at which the option can be exercised.

The cost of making the call

The number of days left until the option is no longer available.

In the event that there are dividends, as well as the total amount of such dividends

When all of these parameters are calculated together, a percentile score can be obtained. The following equation can be used to determine the static rate of return: (Call + Dividend) / Stock Price Time Factor = Static Rate of Return

The if-called return is an approximate annual net profit on a covered call. This profit is based on the expectation that the stock price will be higher than the strike price by the time or on the day the option expires, and that the shares will be sold at the time the option expires. It is necessary to determine the same parameters in order to compute this figure, which is also expressed as a percentage. The following equation can be used to determine this value: (Call plus Dividend) + (Strike minus Stock Price) / Stock Price Time Factor = If-Called Rate of Return

The process of selling real estate is covered in 2.

It's All About Making the Flip

"Flipping" refers to the process of purchasing real estate with the intention of selling it again in a short amount of time for a profit. This particular method of investing in real estate complies with all applicable laws and standards of conduct.

The media's coverage of real estate fraud scenarios, in which someone intentionally overpriced a house, incorrectly falsified documentation, or coordinated with others to take advantage of a buyer, is most likely to blame for the terrible reputation that surrounds real estate flipping. In a genuine flip, none of this would take place.

Finding a house that is suitable for flipping may require a number of risky moves on your part.

You should focus your search on low-cost houses or apartments that require some kind of renovation. You might also try to find a vendor who is motivated to move their inventory quickly and is willing to negotiate a lower price with you.

One strategy for getting leads on property is to talk to people you already know, such as friends, relatives, business acquaintances, real estate brokers, or bankers. Visit the region you are interested in purchasing a home in and look for signs that say "For Sale by Owner" or ring doorbells to see if anyone living there is considering putting their home up for sale.

Investigate the public land records for any "fire sales" that may have occurred. This is typically an indication that the owner of the property is having trouble keeping up with the payments on the mortgage. If you approach them with the intention of selling, and they accept your offer, you will be able to help them get out of a difficult financial situation. In addition to this, you will be purchasing a property that has the potential to bring you a profit. If conducted in a manner that is respectful, this transaction does not involve any immoral behavior.

To become a great real estate flipper, you need to develop a wide variety of skills or polish the ones you already have. You need to have sharp vision to spot the diamond in the rough. You need to have the ability to make an accurate assessment of potential customers. If you are handy and able to undertake even the most basic of house repairs, you will have an advantage. It is essential that you are able to multitask and are attentive to details when managing projects.

Flipping involves a lot of little details, and it's essential to keep on schedule with the job in order to eliminate any unnecessary and expensive delays. Finally, you need to have remarkable skills in dealing with other people.

If you do not already possess this level of knowledge, it is highly recommended that you seek the services of a qualified accountant. Find a reputable attorney who can also provide you with legal guidance and seek their representation.

Understanding the Power of Belief and Putting It to Work is the Topic of Four.

Gaining an understanding of the Infinite Mind, which serves as the foundation of all beings, can be beneficial not just to you but also to humanity. It all boils down to an individual's capacity to maximize not only their own life but also the lives of those in their immediate environment. You can examine Jesus' words now that you have this fresh information and understanding at your disposal. You are going to experience the same level of shock as I did when I realized it. When Jesus talked about having Eternal Life, he meant that his followers should tap into the source of all life, which is the unseen ground that is the Life Force.

"Father who is in heaven."

It was, in point of fact, his Father. This root of being is his father and mother, who are the uncontested source of everything else in the universe. When spring arrives, the appearance of the new sprout that has been dormant in the earth is due to both intelligence and force. If you're reading the Kindle edition on your phone, the animating spirit is what enables you to open and shut your hands around the book as you read. The same power that enables a cheetah to run at speeds of up to sixty miles per hour is responsible for this.

This animate soul is endowed with an intelligence that is both raw and organized. Your mind has the capacity to tap into this energy and use it to organize your experience of the world and make your life easier.

Is it feasible to gain "Eternal Life" by gaining access to the ground of being and learning to work with it in order to fulfill one's potential?

The correct response is "Maybe not eternal, but it seems possible to live to 120, if you can make that mental leap that this book stimulates." Everyone who has been paying attention during the past century is aware of the substantial advancements that have been made in various fields, including medicine, health care, and other areas. This is really fantastic in every way. In affluent countries, the average life expectancy has climbed by a whopping 50 percent. The scientific community is of the opinion that despite the significant progress that has been done, it will take another twenty to thirty years before we can solve the riddles surrounding aging. The process of aging will be halted and possibly even reversed as a result of this discovery. In principle, this will make the possibility of eternal life available.

To the contrary, I believe that anyone who has not made the mental leap that this book can create will have a difficult time achieving the long-term health and vitality that is available to everyone. This is because this book can make a mental leap. They will continue to have the most essential factors that determine aging and disease right in front of them, which is accessible but not invisible, unless they change the way that they think about it.

Take a look at the following cases to see how our mental frames might lead to us missing important details.

During his voyage aboard the Beagle, Charles Darwin made the discovery of Micronesia. Because these islands were so isolated from the rest of the world, the people who lived there had never before witnessed the passage of a ship. Dinghies brought Charles Darwin and the other crew members of the Beagle to the shore. They were not difficult for the indigenous to spot. They were used to sailing on rather modest boats. Even though it was pointed out to them, they could not spot the Beagle docked off the coast, and it is likely that they were unable to see it. They were unable to imagine a boat of this size in their minds. Because of this, they were unable to see it. It is the same today with people becoming older and having health problems. The only way that the majority of people have ever seen the world, and the only way that they see it now, is the manner that conceals it.

This story came about as a result of my realization that denial may be a human characteristic. Because of this mechanism, it will be difficult for certain people to "see" what I am writing about. It is possible to overcome this natural human tendency by practicing willing suspension of disbelief while reading this book and granting yourself permission to engage in serious reflection on what you have read over the course of the next week.

In the spring of the year 2000, after giving a radio interview on one of my books, I had a revelation about something. It was already evening when they arrived. After attempting to amuse and be humorous for sixty minutes, I was completely worn out. On the way home, I stopped at the Seven Eleven near me to pick up a beer. As I got closer to the cash register, I noticed a sign that immediately grabbed my eye.

"We I.D. "We I.D.

I was standing close to a group of adolescents who were enjoying Slurpies. Along with me was a fellow college student, and he stood in my place behind the line. We smiled and said our hellos to one another. It was up to me now. I finished my drink and then went to put the bottle down before reaching for my wallet.

The cashier gave me his attention. She apologized and added, "I'm sorry, but I need to see your identification." "Excuse me?" I asked in return.

She reiterated, "I'm going to need to see my identification," several times.

I responded with, "Are you kidding me?"

She heaved an annoyed and superior sigh out of her mouth. "No, I need to see your ID. I need to see a valid form of identification from you before I can offer you this beer.

I gave her my driver's license, turned around to face my companion, and gave a small shrug in response to her question. Her yawn was quite wide. She cocked her head to the side and then declared, "It's true." "You have a very fresh appearance."

While I was having a drink, I kept an eye out for the police and thought about the fact that I had been requested to provide evidence that I was of an age where it was legal for me to purchase alcohol. At the time, I was fifty-five years old, which was more than twice the age that the clerk demanded to see on my identification. It's true that I had the feeling of being much younger. Even though twenty years have passed, I can still remember virtually exactly how I felt when I was 27 years old.

Following our interaction, I started to ponder the reason(s) why I appeared to be so youthful. After giving it some thought for a bit, the concept of a possibility suddenly occurred to me. I had read a study on people who had been taking enormous levels of vitamin E for more than 10 years, thirty years ago. In the report, the folks had been describing their experiences. The article states that there were no visible indications of aging found in them at all. I purchased a bottle of it, and ever since then I've been making use of it.

For a very long time, I was under the impression that I would never get older. It appeared as though time stood still for me.

After some time, I learned that studies had come to the conclusion that vitamin E in pill form could not be proved to delay the aging process. As is so frequently the case, more recent research frequently disproves prior research. Even yet, it remained something that I had faith in.

Recent publications give the impression that we are quite close to reaching our destination. New research suggests that vitamin E may help reduce the risk of developing heart disease or cancer, in addition to improving your overall health. Although no one is ready to claim that vitamin E may stop the aging process, vitamin E may help minimize the risk of developing these diseases. Despite this, I think the placebo effect was mostly responsible for its success for me back then. It was effective. It was effective. I read an article that said I wouldn't grow old if it was taken away when I was a teenager. That was thirty years ago. It fulfilled its purpose, as I had anticipated it would. If I had read another article suggesting that vitamin E has anti-aging characteristics, I highly doubt that I would have had the same experience.

Belief carries a tremendous amount of power. Placebos have been demonstrated to be effective in a number of studies, including those with blinding procedures. In the field of medicine, a phenomena known as the placebo effect, in which patients report feeling better after ingesting inert substances, has been documented. There have been thousands of clinical trials, hundreds of millions of prescriptions filled, and tens of billions of dollars in sales of antidepressants such as Prozac, Paxil, and Zoloft. One investigation suggests that sugar pills may be just as helpful in treating depression as these medications. According to the findings of certain studies, using a placebo can result in significant brain alterations in the same regions of the brain as are altered by the aforementioned drugs. This study provides irrefutable evidence that the thoughts and beliefs we hold can bring about changes in the physical state of our bodies.

The same body of data also demonstrates that placebos have the potential to outperform the treatments with which they are compared. In a clinical experiment that took place in 2002, it was discovered that St. John's Wort was effective in treating depression in 24 percent of participants. Zoloft was successful in treating 25% of the patients. However, the placebo treatment was successful in entirely curing 32 percent of patients.

When someone takes what they consider to be real medicine, they automatically have certain expectations about the outcomes. In most cases, events turn out the way one anticipated they would. You will learn the reason in this book. For instance, in societies that believe in voodoo or magic, the death toll can be increased by the casting of curses by shamans. A person who does not have faith in the existence of such a curse will not be harmed by it. The outcome is determined by one's expectations of how it will be. This occurrence plays a role in the plot of my book, The Mt. Pelee Redemption, and readers will learn more about it there.

Permit me to relate a genuine account of a case of miraculous recovery. It concerned a woman who I had known for more than a decade at the time it occurred.

Nancy is Nancy's partner in life. The Reverend Tom is Nancy's husband. She has a strong commitment to the beliefs of her religion. A tumor in each of her breasts that measured more than half an inch in diameter was discovered five years ago. Her physician has recommended that she get a biopsy.

A prayer group gathered at her home the night before the operation to pray together. They prayed that the lump wouldn't turn out to be cancerous and that it would go away entirely.

A literal interpretation of the Bible is the basis for Nancy's faith, which takes the Bible very seriously. In Matthew 18:19-20, Jesus made the following statement to his disciples: "I tell you again, if two of us on earth agree about any request you make, it will be done by my Father who is in heaven." Because I am present beside those who have come together in my name.

There were most likely more than two or three of them. It was jam-packed with people. Like me and vitamin E, Nancy anticipated that the prayers would be answered in the affirmative.

Have faith in your own abilities. This belief is essential in order for you to bring your dreams into reality. Learn more. One such illustration can be seen on the Discovery TV Channel, for instance. In this particular instance, two different researchers used the exact identical apparatus to carry out the same ESP experiment. They went to tremendous lengths to ensure that everything was exactly the same, with the exception of one detail. While one of the researchers believed that extrasensory perception (ESP) was real, the other researcher did not. During the testing, there were independent observers present, one of which was a crew from the Discovery Channel TV show.

The investigator who was open to the possibility of extrasensory perception was successful in carrying out an experiment that yielded statistically significant amounts of right scores. This provides evidence that the hypothesis was correctly predicted. The veracity of ESP was demonstrated using scientific methods. Due to the fact that the hits were consistent with the parameters of chance, the experiment with Thomas could not be considered genuine. It would appear that the one and only variable at play here, belief, was what made the difference. The initial researcher had faith, although the latter one did not. Both achieved the effects that he had anticipated.

It is the same thing when Christians pray. Prayer is effective. The act of praying is like letting go of a notion and releasing it into the subconscious. Prayers infuse the spirit, also known as the Life Force, with more energy, which enhances its innate capacity to organize matter in a manner that is advantageous to life. In a short while, it will become abundantly evident to you exactly how this operates, and in Nine, we will discuss in some detail the effects of prayer as proved in scientifically produced and double-blind trials.

Let's begin with Nancy, shall we? Upon further inspection, the lump that Nancy had felt in her breast appeared to have vanished. In order to receive a complete checkup, Nancy remained in the hospital.

The bulge had in fact disappeared. After making the startling discovery that there was no sign of the lump whatsoever, the physician discharged the patient and sent her home.

Is there any way to get rid of the mass of tissue that I have? It was dissolved by the forceful concoction of belief, prayer, and anticipation that was directed toward it. Indeed, we are the creators of our own world. According to the lectures that Thomas Troward, a man who I met for the first time many years ago, has given, this is how it all works. They were introduced for the first time at Queens.

The Edinburgh University Gate was first opened to the public in the year 1904. The conclusions of these lectures, which are known as The Edinburgh Lectures on Mental Science, offer a straightforward and convincing explanation that is consistent with the findings of research on praying. Allow me to break down the structure of prayer for you, despite the fact that it's not particularly complicated.

It is important to begin by considering the distinction between what we consider "dead" stuff and what we recognize as alive material. A sunflower is a plant that stands out because to its one-of-a-kind characteristics. The sunflower will, with its own volition, move its head in the direction of the sun. When first selected, it emits a glowing light. This attribute could also be referred to as the spirit or the life force. It would appear that the piece of steel is absolutely still. However, at the quantum level, the steel has a life of its own. Researchers in quantum physics have demonstrated that every particle of matter is made up of either motion or energy. They cannot be classified as solid substances. They are a source of energy. Strong vibrations. There are others who believe that life can be found anywhere in the universe. It's almost like one gigantic mind, or an intelligence network that's infinitely wide and expansive.

Despite this, the steel gives off the impression of being lifeless even though the sun is still out. The majority of people would agree with this statement. On the other hand, one could make the case that the "aliveness" or condition of being life of a plant is qualitatively distinct from that of an animal. Examine the vivacity of a sunflower, an earthworm, and a goldfish, then compare and contrast their levels of vitality. Each one seems to have a greater sense of life.

Now let's throw in a cat, a toddler, and a stand-up comic who is performing on a late-night talk show. Each one possesses a higher level of intelligence than the previous one. The degree of "aliveness" can be measured, at least to some extent, by either intellect or awareness.

Intelligence, which is often referred to as thought, is the fundamental component that underpins and generates the entire universe. As this intelligence increases its self-awareness, it reveals itself to us more clearly, and our understanding of it improves. The distinguishing feature of life, often known as its spirit, is thought. The chunk of steel exemplifies the fact that shape is the most distinguishing characteristic of matter.

Consider the relationship between mind and shape for a little period. The occupation of space or the constraint of movement within predetermined bounds are two ways to think about form. Both are not implied by thought (or by life). When we picture a concept or a life as being in a particular form, we have a tendency to connect that image with the idea that it takes up space. If we compare an elephant to a mouse, for instance, we might say that the elephant has a bigger volume of live tissue than the mouse. If we consider "aliveness" to be the essential quality of life, then there is no connection between life and the occupation of physical space. The mouse and the elephant both possess the same level of vitality, despite their vastly different sizes. This is a significant point to make. It seems inconceivable that something could exist without taking up space or having any discernible form.

Thought and life do not take up physical space. It is not bound by any era. Time is measured in terms of how long it takes a body to travel from one location in space to another. If there isn't any time, there can't possibly be any space. If cognition and existence are not constrained by space, then they must also not be constrained by time. All thought and life must coexist simultaneously in an endless here and a timeless now, as scientific researchers who have mathematically computed this point would concur.

This sheds light on the operation of prayer and explains how it shapes our experience of the world.

We've already covered the fact that there are two distinct ways of thinking in the conversation that came before. Because the ability to recognize and accept oneself constitutes the defining characteristic of higher-order thought in contrast to lower-order thought, we could refer to these two categories of mind as "lower" and "higher" or "subjective" and "objective." The lower form can only be discovered in plants, worms, and possibly goldfish. They are oblivious to their own identities. It's possible that the comedian and the dog have both. Growing numbers of people have been shown to possess increased levels of self-awareness, much like climbing rungs of a ladder.

Make Sure You Have A Solid Plan Before You Invest Any Money.

I prefer to think of developing a business strategy for investing as similar to ensuring that you are participating in the appropriate league for the sport that you are playing. Keep in mind that the way you invest and the things you invest in are dependent not only on your level of expertise but also the amount of time you have available to invest. When we compare the world of finance to the world of sports, this comparison is actually fairly straightforward. You were born with a natural talent in certain sports, but you are not as skilled in others. You may have been much better at certain sports if you had more time to practice, but due to the fact that you were involved in other activities, you only had a limited amount of time available. This line of reasoning works exactly the same way when applied to investment. You need to ensure that you are capable of outperforming the other swimmers in whichever pool you choose to participate in. If you are continually losing money or exerting an inordinate amount of effort in order to make a pitiful amount of interest, then you are engaging in the incorrect activity. It may take you a little while to figure out what kinds of investments work well for you and which ones don't, and even if it does, if you are doing so, then you are playing the wrong game.

Time in Relation to Profit Ratio

In college, I had a friend who would later have a successful career as a poker player on a professional level. The writing was on the wall; he would constantly spit about his earnings, telling everyone that he won a few hundred here and a few hundred there. It was clear that he was overconfident about his financial situation. Now, you may believe that his life is quite demanding, but you would expect him to have a respectable amount of time to himself. After all, there are only a certain number of poker games that can be played, and simply winning a chosen few may give you a day or two off. This one friend, on the other hand, I think puts in the most hours of anyone I've ever known. People who may benefit from becoming more financially responsible have a tendency to talk incessantly about how much money they are making, but they never discuss the number of hours they put in or the end result of their efforts. This is one of the common characteristics shared by people in this category. It's great that my friend can make a living playing poker, but if he has to put in a hundred stressful hours a week to achieve this goal, I have to wonder if it's really worth it. In order to receive any amount of profit, the precise number of hours that you worked must be listed in the business plan that you have created for your own personal finances. You may have a lot of fun trading foreign currency on the foreign exchange market every day, and you could even make a little money doing it, but if you want to put money away for the future, you need to reevaluate your situation using a cost benefit analysis. Is the amount of time it takes you to choose stocks or invest in the FOREX markets worth the money that you are receiving as a result of these activities? The answer to this question is going to be no for the vast majority of individuals who have full-time employment, but that doesn't mean you shouldn't try your hand at some of these investment opportunities. Simply be prepared to rethink your strategy and have a broad perspective in mind at all times by asking yourself why you are investing.